SOUL REBEL

Soul Rebel

An Intimate Portrait of Bob Marley

David Burnett

Foreword by Chris Salewicz
Introduction by Chris Murray

INSIGHT EDITIONS
San Rafael, California

CONTENTS

"People want to listen to a message, word from Jah. This could be passed through me or anybody. I am not a leader. Messenger. The words of the songs, not the person, is what attracts people."

—BOB MARLEY

FOREWORD *Chris Salewicz*

OB MARLEY WAS A HERO FIGURE, in the classic mythological sense. From immensely humble beginnings with his talent and religious belief as his only weapons, the Jamaican recording artist applied himself with unstinting perseverance to spreading his prophetic musical message. He only departed this planet when he felt his vision of One World, One Love—which was inspired by his belief in Rastafari—was taking root in some quarters. For example, in 1980 the European tour of Bob Marley and the Wailers played to the largest audiences a musical act had up to that point experienced there, the 110,000–strong audience at Milan's San Siro stadium a high point—but it was also one of Bob Marley's final live shows.

On May 11, 1981 he departed this earthly sphere, yet his audience continues, to this day, to widen. To westerners Bob's messianic truths prove inspirational and life-changing, while in developing countries his impact is similar except that its reach extends further. For some, Bob Marley is seen as the Redeemer figure returning to lead this planet out of confusion. Some will come out and say it directly: that Bob Marley is the reincarnation of Jesus Christ long awaited by much of the world. In such an interpretation of his life, the cancer that killed Bob Marley is inevitably described as a modern version of a crucifixion.

Whatever your opinion of this, Bob Marley's story is that of an archetype, which is why it continues to have such a powerful and ever-growing resonance. It embodies, among other themes, political repression, metaphysical and artistic insights, gangland warfare, and various periods in a mystical wilderness. It is no surprise that Bob Marley now enjoys an icon-like status more akin to that of the rebel myth of Che Guevara than to that of a pop star.

Over twenty-five years since his death, thanks to the universal appeal of his prophetic lyrical directness and melodic sweetness, Bob Marley has become almost a modern secular saint because of the global love, loyalty, and fascination that he commands. In these subsequent years, his aptly titled posthumous *Legend* album has sold over fifteen million copies, becoming the biggest selling back catalog album ever in the United States. At present there are almost 800 separate Bob Marley CD releases available worldwide. At the time that the pictures in this book were taken, Bob Marley was readying himself for and then taking part in the tour for the *Exodus* album, a series of dates and a record that saw his greatness stamped forever on our culture.

Exodus is a masterful record, but then Bob Marley never really wrote a bad song. The music and lyrics that have uplifted the world began to be written in Jamaica's Trench Town when he was an early teenager. His work, even the very sound of it, was a product of his healthy country upbringing colliding with the shockingly harsh reality of urban ghetto life. His antennae tuned to suffering and oppression, Bob Marley turned his experiences into words of universal truth.

When you first heard it, the music of Bob Marley and The Wailers struck you as sounding utterly otherworldly. Adding to that sense of strangeness, *Catch a Fire*, his first album on Island Records, also contained tinges of psychedelia, a hangover from the musicians' then recent work with Lee "Scratch" Perry. The songs could be angry, sweet, or joking which were all aspects of Bob Marley's wonderful personality, and the highly intelligent musician sought out that balance on his records. As the years have progressed the music that once sounded so odd has become part of the soundtrack of modern life.

Bob was born Robert Nesta Marley on February 6, 1945 in the inland Jamaican hamlet of Nine Miles, in the parish of St Ann's, also the birthplace of Marcus Garvey, the black prophet and proselytizer of Pan-Africanism. Although himself not strictly a Rastafarian, it was Garvey who memorably urged his followers to look to the crowning of a new king in Africa who, he insisted, would prove to be of divine origin. Shortly after Marcus Garvey had made this prophetic utterance, in 1930 Haile Selassie I was crowned Emperor of Ethiopia, King of Kings, Conquering Lion of the Tribe of Judah.

Although inland St Ann's is a region of rolling tropical hills and lushly verdant valleys, in which ganja plantations may be secreted with ease, Nine Miles was a desperately poor, agricultural village. The home in which he grew up, his mother's one-room stone hut, had no electricity or running water, a pile of stones for a stove, and an outhouse. It was also an area known for its mystical associations in which *obeah* —Jamaican voodoo, an offshoot of African animist religions —played a strong part, often interlinked with Baptist strains of Christianity. This amorphous blend hints at the imprecise and anarchic nature of Rastafari—of which Bob Marley would come globally to be seen as the personification.

Bob Marley has also become almost synonymous with the strange and mystical island of Jamaica with whose destiny he was so inextricably bound. Bob was the product of a colonial island that had come to independence in 1962. His life mirrored the struggles of an emergent nation which, in the second half of the 1970s, was plunged into the horror of an undeclared civil war. He came to symbolize Jamaican culture when, in April 1978, the One Love Peace Concert was held in Kingston at Bob Marley's instigation with the intention of drawing the opposing factions together. Events such as these also brought Bob Marley to the attention of the CIA, who kept copious files on the man dubbed "the first Third World superstar."

Jamaica is a complex collision of cultural diversities. The national motto is "Out of Many, One People." Jamaica's identity is formed from not only a heritage of African slaves and indentured laborers from England, Ireland, India, and China, as well as the island's original Arawak Indians, but from the entire belief systems brought by these new arrivals. A legacy of rebellion was fermented in Jamaica by the Maroons, slaves who had escaped to the Blue Mountains to form a rebel army that regularly defeated the English redcoats. At that time plantations were attacked as frequently as a U.S. frontier cavalry post. Contemporaneously, the island became the world capital of piracy. Until it was flung into the Caribbean in an earthquake in 1692, the then capital of Port Royal, whose fortune was built largely on piracy, was known as "the wickedest place on earth." Is it any wonder that this tropical island seems like a microcosm of a concentrated, exaggerated strain of humanity? Or that Bob Marley would stridently announce on record his position as a "Soul Rebel"?

Struggling to emerge from the dangerous and dramatic cultural soup of his origins, the young Robert Nesta Marley seemed to have been born with a poet's understanding of the mysteries of life. In Nine Miles by the age of five he was already a respected reader of palms.

Clearly Bob's family background is of paramount importance in understanding him. Bob was born to a black Jamaican mother and a white Jamaican father, Captain Norval Marley, a captain in the British West India Regiment, who twice abandoned him. Bob Marley's negative relationship experiences while he was a child were played out in relationships with others for the rest of his life. With no significant male role model, he constantly sought out surrogate figures such as Joe Higgs, the Trenchtown music teacher, Mortimer Planner, the Rasta elder, and Chris Blackwell, who bankrolled Bob's success through his Island Records. His relationship with his father was always complex. Was the young man later calling out "One Love" to the world quietly desperate for any kind of love or validation?

His complex relationships with women also attest to a dysfunctional upbringing, one that evidently fuelled his art. Years later, Rita Marley, his wife, would try to explain away to me Bob's ceaseless philandering by claiming, "He was just looking for love everywhere—anywhere he could find it, because he'd never had it." Did Bob Marley also need to be vindicated by the love of concert audiences and record buyers everywhere?

Within the first five years of Bob Marley's life he would again experience rejection and trauma when his father spirited him away, allegedly to live with him in the rough Jamaican capital of Kingston, but in fact to be lodged with a kind of ghetto governess. His father then disappeared for the second and final time in Bob's life. Separated from both his mother and father, the young boy found salvation in that time through discovering his vocal talents. He was rescued by his mother by chance after a neighbor from Nine Miles noticed him on the downtown Kingston streets.

Moving semi-permanently from the country to Kingston when he was ten, times at first were rough. But through his friendship with Bunny Livingstone (with whose father Bob's mother was in a relationship) and then Peter Tosh, he began to find himself with their group, The Wailers. By 1964, releasing singles on the revered Studio One label, The Wailers were one of the biggest acts in Jamaica—though on the cash-strapped island this did not translate into financial benefit.

In Trench Town Bob Marley found a mentor in Mortimer Planner, a revered Rasta elder who became his manager, caring for Bob when he underwent a creative crisis that manifested as a minor nervous breakdown. In 1968 Bob was with Planner when he met Danny Sims, a music business entrepreneur who managed Johnny Nash, a Texas-born singer who was to have his first substantial U.S. chart success the next year with "Hold Me Tight." Bob signed his publishing to Sims' Cayman Music outfit and struck a deal for recording with his JAD label. Sims put Bob on a weekly wage of fifty U.S. dollars.

Bob and The Wailers, however, continued to record for themselves and other producers. After working with Leslie Kong on a few singles, The Wailers linked up with another disaffected member of the Lloyd Coxsone camp, Lee "Scratch" Perry. Scratch, a former "selector" for Coxsone's sound system, had set up his own label named after another of his nicknames, "The Upsetter." He was an early exploiter of the new sound of reggae, which was fast overtaking the slowed-down beat of rock steady that had emerged in the summer of 1966. Most importantly, his rhythm section of drummer Carlton Barrett and his bass-playing brother Aston "Family Man" Barrett clicked with The Wailers. Soon they joined the group, recording a pair of extraordinary LPs with Scratch Perry producing. At the core of these records was an approach to the music that was more like that of a rock act—a pointer to the future.

In 1970, under the auspices of Danny Sims, Bob found himself in Stockholm, Sweden, working with Johnny Nash on the soundtrack of a movie in which Nash was starring. Afterwards Bob flew to London where a full-scale tour was set up for The Wailers. For this tour, however, the group was booked into inappropriate venues, secondary schools in the middle of the country, for example, and the group ended up in a studio in London, working with Johnny Nash on his LP, *I Can See Clearly Now*. This was to contain three Bob Marley compositions, one of which, "Stir It Up," would become a big hit single.

After the sessions, however, the group found themselves stranded in the English capital. On the advice of Brent Clarke, a radio plugger, the group got in touch with Chris Blackwell, a white Jamaican who ran Island Records, the most successful British-based independent label. Blackwell had been warned that The Wailers were trouble and said, "But in my experience when people are described like that, it usually just means that they know what they want." Blackwell cut a deal with them. He would give them £4,000 to return to Jamaica and make an LP. When he received the final tapes they would get another £4,000. Blackwell was quoted as saying, "Everyone told me I was mad: they said I'd never see the money again." On their return to Jamaica, The Wailers immediately went into Kingston's Dynamic Studio. By the end of the year the album, *Catch A Fire*, was completed.

And so continued the process. In China you can hear Bob Marley, but not Bruce Springsteen, and this is replicated globally. In the most obscure bush hamlet in the African interior you will come across murals of "The First Third World Superstar," especially in those parts of West Africa from which slaves were plucked and taken to the New World. Australia's aborigines, New Zealand's Maoris, and America's Hopis regard him with saint-like reverence. In the countries of the former Soviet Bloc Bob Marley was seen by the youth as a light to lead them from darkness. In more recent years he has been taken up as an archetypal icon by the American world of hip-hop.

Today Bob Marley's name and image resonate around the globe, the personification of conscious thought and consideration towards one's fellow humans.

CHRIS SALEWICZ

"Behold, how good and how
pleasant it is for brethren to
dwell together in unity!"

—Psalm 133

INTRODUCTION *Chris Murray*

It's not every day that you come across an unpublished collection of photographs of a legend.
It is even more amazing when those photographs were taken by an accomplished, award-
winning photojournalist. That is indeed the case with the photographs in this book by David
Burnett. Taken on assignment in Jamaica for *Time* in 1976, only two of Burnett's photographs were
published to accompany the story by reporter David DeVoss, and only one of them was of Bob
Marley. A year later, Burnett photographed Marley again, this time on the Exodus Tour in Europe
for *Rolling Stone*. Those two assignments led Burnett to making some of the finest photographic
portraits ever taken of the charismatic international superstar.

Both Bob Marley and David Burnett were in their early thirties when they met at Marley's
home on Hope Road in Kingston, Jamaica. In a number of ways they were kindred spirits. Both
of them were young men who were telling stories through their respective mediums, music and
photography, and they had both seen their share of suffering.

David Burnett began his journey as a photographer in 1962 in Salt Lake City, Utah, taking
pictures for his high school yearbook; far from Trenchtown, where Bob Marley grew up. Burnett
worked in a camera store in the summer during his breaks from high school. He liked to go to drag
races on weekends and would shoot pictures of the cars and drivers. After the races, he would go
home and make prints in the darkroom he built in the furnace shed of his parents' house. He would
then sell the prints to the racecar drivers for $1.50 each. He realized early on that he could make
money with a camera and that he wanted to be a photographer.

Burnett went on to study political science at Colorado College, and during this time his interest
in photography deepened. He became influenced by the work of photographers Robert Capa,
Henri Cartier-Bresson, and David Douglas Duncan. During his college summer breaks, Burnett
interned at *Time* in New York and Washington, D.C. *Time* staff photographer Walter Bennett took
Burnett under his wing. He taught the young and ambitious photographer: "First of all, don't waste
people's time. And the second thing is to get the damned picture. And sometimes, the second thing
is more important than the first."

After graduating from college, Burnett went to work for *Time*. In 1969, he traveled to Jamaica to cover a story on the Black Power Movement in the Caribbean. The following year, Burnett bought a ticket to Saigon. He went on to cover the war in Vietnam for two years for *Life*. Burnett was twenty-four years old and found himself in Vietnam during the invasion of Laos. He was also there during the "Easter Offensive" and related that "the North Vietnamese nearly took it all."

Burnett found himself in any number of fire-fights. He was with photographer "Nick" Ut at Trang Bang when the most famous photo from that war was taken of a young naked Vietnamese girl running desperately down the road, fleeing a Napalm explosion.

After Vietnam, Burnett went to work for the French photo agency Gamma, traveling throughout the world on assignments. His photographs were being published in the *New York Times*, *Geo*, *Time*, the *New Yorker*, and numerous other publications. It was during this period that Burnett took the assignment from *Time* with reporter David DeVoss to cover the reggae scene in Jamaica.

Burnett and DeVoss began their trip in Ocho Rios with Burnett photographing various "North Shore" reggae groups, including Burning Spear, Foundation, and Ras Michael. After a few days in Ocho Rios, they went to Kingston, where Burnett was able to photograph Peter Tosh, a recording session with Burning Spear, Lee "Scratch" Perry, and Bob Marley.

It wasn't very long after Burnett sat and "reasoned" with Marley in his home in Kingston that Bob Marley was shot in a failed assassination attempt. Marley's personal manager, Don Taylor, was hit by a number of bullets. Marley's wife, Rita, was shot in the head. Marley was hit by a bullet in the arm.

Miraculously, no one was killed. It was only a few months later, during the summer of 1977, that Burnett joined Bob Marley and The Wailers on their bus in Europe during the Exodus Tour. Burnett photographed Marley and the band on the bus, during sound check, playing soccer, and in concert. Taken only a year after his first sessions with Marley, this time Burnett was well aware that he was documenting an international superstar—a unique artist at the height of his abilities.

I asked David Burnett one day what his first-hand impression of Bob Marley was after having the opportunity to photograph him in a number of different circumstances. Burnett thought quietly to himself for a minute and then told me this: "Some things you're born with, and some things you can acquire. But with someone like Bob Marley, he was definitely born with it ... and it is something that grew from within."

Bob Marley will always remain one of the most beloved and respected musical artists of our time. His is the music of liberation and love. It speaks of redemption. It is sung from the heart and is driven by a mesmerizing rhythm and a universal beat. Marley's performances were legendary. He danced as if possessed by a higher calling. His artistry evokes the magic and mysteries of the ancients ... the dreadlocked rasta.

David Burnett's photographs take us to the soul of Bob Marley, Jamaica, and its people. His photographs will long be remembered for honoring that soul.

One Love,
CHRIS MURRAY
Washington, D.C.

ABOVE: Lee "Scratch" Perry at his studio

1

OCHO RIOS

"Soon the earth will tilt on
its axis and begin to dance
to the reggae beat to the
accompaniment of earthquake.
And who can resist the dance
of the earthquake, mon?"
—PETER TOSH

In 1976, I had been working for *Time* magazine for about eight years. I had a
good relationship with the picture editors there, and they would occasionally call me for
some interesting stories. David DeVoss, a reporter who lived in L.A., was the *Time* Hollywood
correspondent, and he was plugged in to the music business as well as the film business. When
Island Records decided to invite some mainstream publications in, he was the guy *Time* went to
and I joined him in Ocho Rios, Jamaica. Island Records was holding the hands of half a dozen
journalists trying to explain to them a little bit about reggae music and who the players were. A
number of reggae musicians were recording with Island Records. We spent three or four days in
Ocho Rios.

We had heard about Bob Marley, but no one I knew was really familiar with reggae, and it
wasn't something I had much personal knowledge of. But when we got to Jamaica, our first few
nights they had groups come and sing at the hotel. Photographer Peter Simon was also there. I
remember having some strobe lights, which I put up in the hotel club. Our little hotel had a very
low ceiling, and you couldn't really bounce the strobes up high enough—but it was so dark that you
needed some light just to see anything. I let Peter—and anybody else who was there—use them.
Burning Spear and several other groups were the ones we heard perform.

Island Records figured Ocho Rios was a nice place to start our trip, because Kingston was
still a rough town. Island did a good job looking after us. The whole trip had to do with how as
Americans we interpret this music and what the messages are. Reggae wasn't just another brand
of rock and roll. It had its own particular roots, an evolution from earlier Jamaican forms of music
such as ska and rock steady, which had morphed into the birth of reggae. It was a word we'd all
sort of heard, kicked around, but nobody really knew much about what it meant. So I got lucky
and was tapped for the story, and it was great. I had been to Jamaica before, in 1969, when I'd gone
there to do a story on Black Power and politics in the Caribbean.

In the beginning, the whole thing struck me as a curious new form of music that I had not
been exposed to. So it was interesting to hear, and if you could take time to slow down enough and
listen to what they were singing, the lyrics were always good, provocative. It's funny—it was easy to
feel a little bit like an idiot because we didn't know who was important and who wasn't. Sometimes
the people who looked like they ought to be the important ones weren't, and the ones that looked
least likely to be important turned out to be the big movers. I had heard of Marley. I knew about
him. Burning Spear—you know, people told me about him. They would take me aside and say,
"Oh, you really need to listen to these guys." ✸

OPPOSITE: Burning Spear

ABOVE: Ras Michael and the Sons of Negus (L: Ras Sidney; R: Kiddus I)

PREVIOUS PAGE; ABOVE: Burning Spear
ABOVE RIGHT: The Black Disciples, Spear's band. Top L to R: Vin Gordon,
Noel "Zoot" or "Scully" Simms, Richard "Dirty Harry" Hall, Earl "Chinna"
Smith; bottom L to R: Robbie Shakespeare, Bobby Ellis, Herman Marquis,
Bernard Harvie, Leroy "Horsemouth" Wallace

TOP: Maurice Robert (R) with the Dexter Brothers

ABOVE: Ras Michael & the Sons of Negus (L: Ras Sidney; R: Kiddus I)

OPPOSITE: Jammin' at producer Jack Ruby's house in Ocho Rios

2

KINGSTON

"Maybe them [the Jamaican government] go nationalize reggae next. Them didn't use to like it, but reggae is the people's music . . . . Them going have to do something, or the people going burn this place down."

—Bob Marley

After a few days in Ocho Rios, we decided to go to Kingston. We

wanted to see Bob and hang around for a couple of days, and try to get a sense of what the place was like and what the politics were that gave rise to the music we were hearing. The first time I went into Trench Town, I started to get an idea of why they were writing the music. It was pretty bad: rough and very intimidating. There were two political parties, the People's National Party (PNP) headed by Michael Manley, who was at that time the Prime Minister of Jamaica. Then there was the head of the opposition, Edward Seaga of the Jamaica Labour Party (JLP). Things were very clearly defined. If you were PNP, you didn't drive into a JLP area and vice versa. Things got really nasty. There were a lot of shootings. Politics was a form of blood sport in Jamaica.

The movie *The Harder They Come* had been released a couple of years earlier, and one afternoon in Ocho Rios we met the director Perry Henzell. I got a few pictures of him down on the beach near the hotel. Jimmy Cliff was probably the best-known Jamaican singer at the time because he was the star of *The Harder They Come*. That movie brought reggae music and the culture of Kingston to many people's attention for the first time.

In Kingston, we went to some record stores, and then hung out that afternoon at a recording studio, the same time, as it turned out, that Burning Spear was recording there. That was pretty cool. Randy's Record Store was the name of the place, and I think the studio was attached to it. It was owned by Randy Chin, who was from a Chinese-Jamaican family. I went in there, and these guys were trying to put it together to make a song. There's one really good photo of everybody gathered around the piano, and one guy just kind of laid out on the bench with a spliff in his hands. We heard them harmonizing and doing their thing. It was like watching a song being born.

After we left the recording studio, David and I went to see Peter Tosh. David had an interview with him for about 30 to 40 minutes, and then I had maybe 20 minutes to shoot pictures. Peter Tosh was a cool dude. The thing is, with all of these guys, there was no namby-pambying around. They knew what they wanted, they knew what I wanted to do, they knew what their capabilities were, and they just didn't want any bullshit. They just wanted to get down to it. They could be running occasionally on Caribbean time, which meant a rendezvous could start late, but that's something you just got used to. They were all pretty forthright. "Legalize it and I'll advertise it." Peter Tosh was very right there with it. He was trying to get people to legalize it.

31

kingston

PREVIOUS PAGE: Peter Tosh in Kingston
OPPOSITE: Singer Rupert Willington relaxing during a Burning Spear recording session
ABOVE: Film director Perry Henzell

After photographing Tosh, we went to see the producer Lee "Scratch" Perry. He was a wild and crazy guy, and I mean that in a good sense. He was not on the same charts I was on. He understood the music and where it was coming from and what it represented for society. He was a one-man operation, trying to help people create music and churn it out there.

Even for David, the reporter, it was pretty much our first serious exposure to reggae music. David had been listening to some reggae recordings as part of his story preparation. I wouldn't be surprised if he had been sent a bunch of records and had been playing them. But I didn't know much of the music until I got down to Jamaica. It was really out of the blue for me.

As a photographer I operate on the principle that there are a whole bunch of interesting people out there that I just haven't gotten a chance to meet yet. That's what makes photography so much fun. You could go in any direction, from music or politics to literary figures and athletes. It was all interesting and a real learning and discovery process. Coming in knowing nothing about it, you were starting at square one and trying to understand not just a person, but also a little bit about the culture that spawned the person and that brought along the music.

Though I had been down to Jamaica a couple of times on political stories in the late 1960s and early 1970s, I didn't really know that much about the country. Jamaica was always a tough place, and now you had all the AK-47 and M-16 boys. It feels like everybody is armed. But the culture is such that it has created some amazing artists. You can see the expression of a lot of that in Marley's case, growing up in Trench Town and what that was all about. It didn't take very long before you understood that his was a creative, interesting voice from that culture. And not only that, the music was great, the lyrics were interesting, and what I love about Jamaica is that because it has

kind of grown up in its own little cauldron, the language is so descriptive and wonderful. It's not like speaking English with anybody else. They have their own way of talking and using English words and adding things to them, and it's just fabulous and richly descriptive.

When I worked on a *National Geographic* story about Jamaica, one of the things that I loved were these little encounters with people, whether they were ministers or a farmer with a shovel out in the middle of a field. You could have the most colorful and amazing conversation, and the language was so very rich and personal. It could be tough, but there was always an edge of humor in there, which was what I came to really like about the country. Even people who might shout at you for taking their picture, after a while if you stay and engage them, they admire the fact that you didn't just run off, and you could have a great conversation. There were a couple of times when I couldn't get past that anger, but I had the most wonderful, amazing conversations and encounters with people that I've probably ever had on an assignment.

When we took on the story for *Time,* there were only a few really well known reggae musicians. *The Harder They Come* was a window on Jamaica at a time when most outsiders had never bothered paying any attention to the place, other than as a possible destination to go to for a suntan. I haven't seen the movie for 30 years, but there are still a few lines in there, they just keep coming back at me. "Why he get dead?" You know, not, "Why did he die?" "Why he get dead?" People were taking the same basic building blocks and the same sets of words we all share, but creating a whole new language out of it and doing it in a way that is very poetic and captivating, and maybe very simple, but there is an artistry in the way that happens. ✺

ABOVE: Producer Clive Chin lights a cigarette

TOP: Burning Spear

ABOVE: Jack Ruby (bearded, center) and musicians during the session

PREVIOUS PAGE; ABOVE & OPPOSITE: Peter Tosh

ABOVE & OPPOSITE: Lee "Scratch" Perry at his studio

ABOVE: Outside Lee "Scratch" Perry's studio, L to R: Mickey Boo,
Max Romeo, Lee, Clancy Eccles, Chinna Smith
OPPOSITE: Scratch at the mixing board with Max

ABOVE: Noel "Zoot" or "Scully" Simms and Lee "Milo" Spence at Jack
Ruby's in Ocho Rios
RIGHT: Hanging out in Trench Town, and the Gun Court, Kingston

3

TUFF GONG

"Here was a man [Bob Marley] who loved his roots . . . and knew they extended to the ends of the earth."
—ALICE WALKER

Our assignment was about reggae, and Bob Marley was THE man. We had secured an interview with Bob. The interview was arranged by people from Island Records, and we were told to show up at a certain time in the early afternoon. We spent several hours there. Bob couldn't have been more charming and open and just willing to engage—the dialogue of "reasoning." I mean, we were just talking it through.

Bob's home was a compound. There was a big, old colonial house and a few smaller buildings, a beautiful place. DeVoss and I went in and walked around a bit. When we sat down for the interview, it was in a room upstairs. It's funny because today you would say, well, I've got to go and bring in my lights tripod, etc. But this was just walk in and there's the window, and Bob sits down, and there was just enough window light to take pictures.

We sat on the floor and just started talking. David turned on his tape recorder, and we were there with Bob for well over an hour. David was one of these guys who had reported from 25 or 30 countries and was wounded in Vietnam when he was a *Time* correspondent during the war. He had become one of *Time's* Hollywood correspondents, mostly doing film and music.

I knew David from Vietnam, and we had done a number of other stories together. He was a very soft-spoken kind of guy. It was interesting, because his interviewing technique would be to just kind of throw something out there, to just tee it up for you. He is a Texan, so he had a little bit of that slowly metered Southern way of speaking. "Well, they told me so and so and so and so. What do you think?" It wasn't one of these "gonna get you" kinds of interviews. It was a very soft conversation, with all kinds of very interesting topics. Bob talked about the Rastafari movement and what the role of ganja was in that movement. He talked about music and expression and how that relates to the life that he had growing up, and what Jamaica is about now. Bob was a very smart guy. When he said something, there was always weight behind it. It wasn't just sort of thrown off because it's an interview, let's get it over with. It was a very engaging time while we were there, a very wide-ranging interview.

Here's a guy, Bob Marley, who grew up in circumstances way different than either David DeVoss or I could ever imagine, and he's arrived at this transcendent place. For a young man, he had a lot of wisdom. For someone like myself who had spent, at that point, ten years traveling the world, working in many different situations, and as a photojournalist just trying to capture what's out there, my approach was not to go in and lay my point of view over what was there, beyond some stylistic touches. I wanted to report what I saw. While I thought I was pretty experienced for 31 years old, at the same time, when you meet somebody who's so articulate, you're thinking, God, this is really extraordinary. Here's a person who can actually put into words, and with a really interesting phraseology, thoughts that are way beyond what I'd been thinking about. My expression is almost all subconscious and unconsciously done through the camera. So when you hear someone who can so clearly say what he thinks and feels, you pay attention.

During the interview, Bob lit up a number of spliffs. There was a sense of hospitality. You know, he would just light it up and pass it around; and you took a hit. That's not one you turn down. And we were not only journalists, we were perfect guests. On the hospitality level, I try never to embarrass myself as a guest.

What is always interesting to see is the impact that certain people can have. I was thinking of what Abe Lincoln said to Harriet Beecher Stowe, the author of *Uncle Tom's Cabin*: "So you're the little woman who wrote the book that started this great war." Bob Marley was not imposing in terms of his physical being. It was much more the sense of being in the presence of a smart and very talented artist. As I look back

on all the people I've photographed who have caused these brouhahas, I wonder about them and what made them who they are. Here's just a kid from Trench Town who started playing the guitar and who knew he had a mission. He lived in a very tough environment, which certainly influenced a lot of his views.

So over the course of the interview, in one ear I'm sort of trying to tune out and just think, well, "how's the light," you know, from the photographic side, and the other ear is listening to all this stuff and trying to figure out, based on what he might have just said, what kind of expression I want. What kind of expression am I waiting for, to get a picture that's going to bounce back to what he's saying? And that's one of those things that as it's happening, you're listening and trying to immediately process what you've just heard into some visual photographic reinterpretation. There were no bombshells in the interview. There wasn't anything that would make your jaw drop. But it was just a really interesting discussion, and at the same time, there I am, writing with my camera, trying to figure out, based on what I'm hearing, how I can get some little moment, what kind of a portrait will give a little insight into what he's about.

After the interview, we went outside to the compound yard. When you do these kinds of interviews, part of it is for the text, and part of it has got to be for the pictures. It's good to work with writers like David DeVoss who understand that their stories have a better chance of working and being published if you have good pictures. At the same time, I understand that they really need a good interview for this story to run. It can't just be about the pictures. You want the whole process to go well. You want your writer, your partner, to come up with

ABOVE: Bob Marley and David DeVoss

material that would be able to be written in a way that's going to make your editors feel compelled to run it. Too often you get people who are so concentrated on their own work that they don't think of that other side. But it is words and pictures, and that's kind of what makes it work together.

Bob brought his guitar outside, and I noticed that he had taken scissors and cut out a picture of Haile Selassie (Jah Rastafari) and taped it right on the guitar. It wasn't like, send it down to the guitar photo shop and have this mounted on the guitar. It had much more of the feeling of something that was done—just some afternoon he decided to do it—and he cut the picture out and taped it on, and it's been there for some time. I said, let me get a shot of you with Jah Rastafari himself, and he was perfectly obliging and happy to do it.

Since I had brought along my "slit" camera, I asked Bob to start running with the guitar from left to right, in front of the camera. He did it once, and, eventually I think I got him to do it about nine or ten more times. He wondered what that was about. It's not as if we were yet in the digital age. You can't just show somebody the screen on the back of the camera with what you've just done. There's a certain leap of faith that has to go along with this, and I think at least he felt it was worth trying, if I was making such a big deal out of it.

I told Bob: "This is a weird little camera, and you need to actually be running in order for the picture to be sharp, because everything that's stationary is going to be blurry. It doesn't make sense, but the film is moving, and you're moving, so we're going to try to lay your image down right on the film." And I think about the third sentence, when you try to explain this to anybody, they're just kind of like, "Why don't we just do it?"

I had not yet developed the "slit" camera technique to the point that I absolutely knew I was going to get a picture out of it. And I'm doing it by hand, and I'm trying to uncover the lens … It was totally half-assed, yet the picture was pretty cool. A year later, when I was with Bob on the bus in Europe during the Exodus tour, one of the French magazines had run that "slit" camera picture. I showed him the magazine, and he immediately knew what the deal was. He looked at it, and I said, "Remember when I had you run back and forth by the garage?" And he just started smiling. "That's it, you know." And he said, "Very cool," because he really dug the fact that this was something that he'd never seen before, a bit of a different view of him. So it was fun, because he was pretty willing to do anything, and you can tell when you've pretty much worn people out, you know, running 20 feet back and forth with a guitar.

We must have been at the compound for several hours. When you consider today that if you get seven minutes for an interview and all the little PR minions are standing around in their cocktail dresses, tapping their feet—I mean, this was really a pretty nice little gig. If you try to get that kind of time with somebody now, unless it's really something they want to do, it's extremely difficult, and especially to just see them as they are.

When we returned to the U.S.A., I went to *Time*, and they published the story. They only ran two small black and white pictures. But even in those days, if you had a page or a page-and-a-half story in *Time* magazine, 20 million people would see it that week. And it was not a story that had made the evening news, and it was unlikely to be on Cronkite and CBS before it was published in *Time*. In those days, the news magazines still had a very big impact on people. The whole point about *Time* and *Newsweek*, even up through the seventies, was that if you spent an hour reading them, you would know everything that you needed to know about what was happening in the world that week. ☻

7603 A 27

→0A   →1   →1A   →2   →2A   →3   →3A   →4   →4A

→5   →5A   →6   →6A   →7   →7A   →8   →8A   →9   →9A

→10   →10A   →11   →11A   →12   →12A   →13   →13A   →14A

→15   →15A   →16   →16A   →17   →17A   →18   →18A   →19   →19A

→20   →20A   →21A   →22   →22A   →23   →23A   →24   →24A

→25   →25A   →26   →26A   →27   →27A   →28   →28A   →29   →29A

→30   →30A   →31   →31A   →32   →32A   →33   →33A   →34A

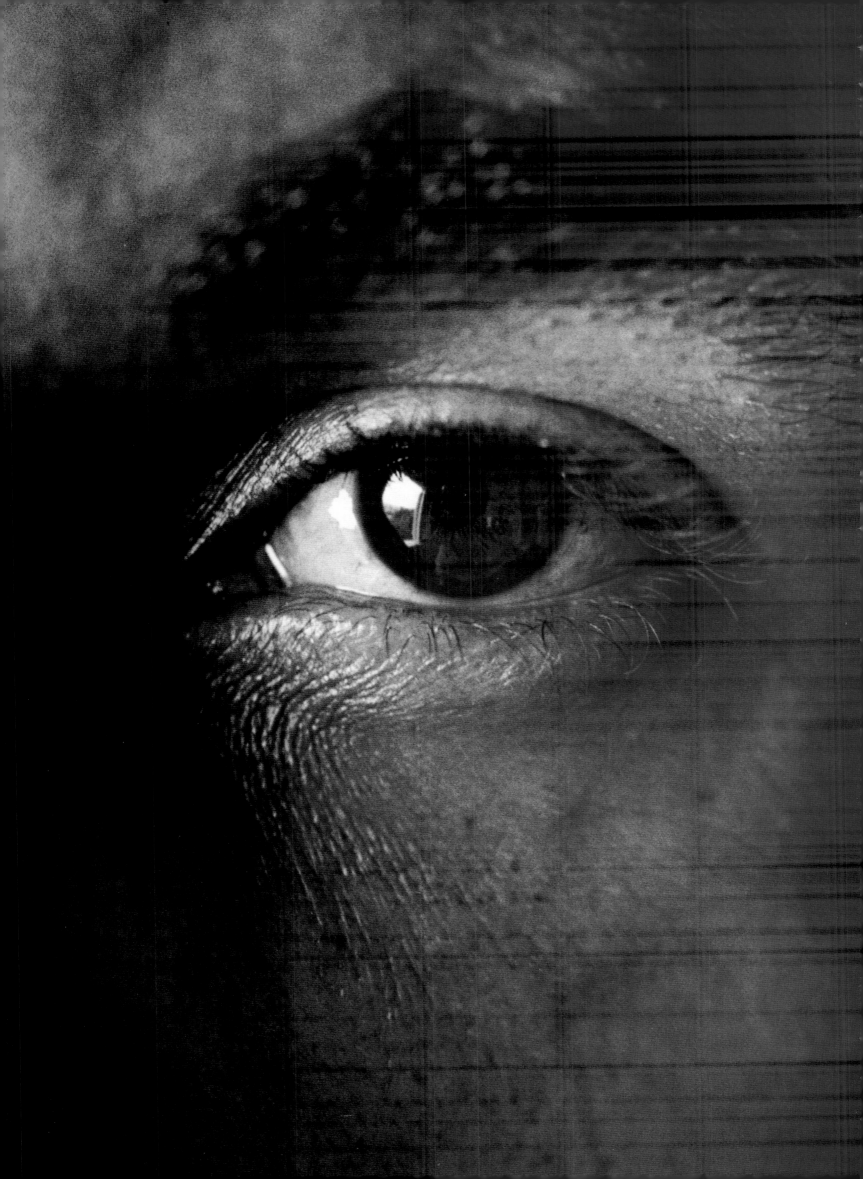

4

EXODUS TOUR

"Marley is a blur of motion, bobbing, weaving, dreadlocks flying, never seeming to quite touch the stage."

—Robert Palmer

About a year later, I was in Paris and a call came to join Bob Marley and The Wailers on a road trip for a few days during the Exodus tour for *Rolling Stone*. That seemed like a great idea to me! By then I knew that these guys were a pretty big deal. I jumped at the opportunity when I got the call to go do the story. I was living in Paris from about February to August of '77, crashing at a friend's apartment. Looking back on it, I must say my friend was very understanding about having somebody sleep in his living room for that long. I was there six months. I also was gone a lot but still, it was a big favor. It put me in a place where an opportunity like this one with Bob Marley and The Wailers for *Rolling Stone* could happen.

I'd gone over to Europe do a story with Kurt Waldheim, the Secretary General of the United Nations. I'd been working in the Middle East, had come back to Vienna and then gone on to Paris. Once I got to Paris, things just started happening. That was the summer that I went to Ethiopia. I also went to Spain twice to do a story on that country after Franco, and another one on La Pasionaria, a woman who had been a communist leader during the Spanish Civil War. I did assignments in Italy and Yugoslavia. I was working all the time. It was a great summer. Joining the bus on the Exodus tour was part of that summer.

Our itinerary included Amsterdam, Brussels, and Paris. It was really cool when they did their sound checks. Everyone in the band was up on the stage and there was no sound other than their playing music while I'm shooting my pictures. And you knew that in six hours there were going to be 30,000 kids down there, but right now there are just six people.

Somebody always had a soccer ball, and if there was a lull in the action, man, they'd just be kicking that ball around, and that was the way they enjoyed hanging out.

I like the sequence of Bob sleeping on the bus. He was napping, getting comfortable, watching the Dutch countryside blow by. The band was pretty cool about me. They knew that I was able to deliver the pictures and they had seen the photos I had taken of them published. They never said, don't do this or don't do that. They were truly welcoming.

There's nothing like live music and hearing it in a big venue and with a big sound system. During the shows, I had good access. The concerts were very energetic. Bob Marley and The Wailers were huge stars in Europe, so everywhere they went, it was a packed house, and people were really into them and really into the music.

It wasn't a madhouse on stage. They were just into the music, and the music was really what it was about, and you're live, it's a lot of horsepower, and you're just bathed in the music. It's nothing like being at home and turning your stereo up as loud as it goes. When there's this much amplification and the speakers are that big, the sound just kind of goes through your body. The mass of it, you feel it in your whole body. It isn't just listening to it; you're feeling it. And their songs, there's a lot of that real heavy bass side, and everybody in the audience is just moving. They may not be moving so much on stage, but, boy, the audience, they're all cranking. The music was great. The lyrics were great. It is always a treat when you get to hear great music and that was the best reggae music there was. 🖼

OPPOSITE: With the I-Three (Rita Marley, Judy Mowatt, Marcia Griffiths)

OPPOSITE TOP: Alvin "Secco" Patterson and Aston "Family Man" Barrett
OPPOSITE BOTTOM: Tyrone Downie
ABOVE: Road Manager Tony "Gilly" Gilbert

ABOVE: Bob Marley with photographer Kate Simon

ACKNOWLEDGEMENTS *David Burnett*

When you take thirty years to get around to doing a project, you hope it ends up right. I had the pleasure of spending some time in Jamaica discovering the insights and joys of reggae in 1976. A year later, I traveled with Bob and The Wailers in Europe for a week. It was a time when a photographer could still get close to his subjects, before today's era of "handlers," press agents, and PR mavens who seem to see their job as providing endless blockage and interruption. There is nothing like the real thing when you are taking pictures. I'm grateful for having had the chance to spend that time, with camera in hand and sometimes without.

I've known Chris Murray of Govinda Gallery for twenty years. Last year, when I brought him the photographs for the first time, he lit up with enthusiasm. "Where have you kept these?" he asked. Like all my pictures of the last forty years, they reside at my agency, Contact Press Images, in New York, where they've been in and out of numerous magazines for years, often greeted with the remark: "These ought to be a book." Chris agreed wholeheartedly and took the project to heart. We looked at the material many times, and distilled it down to what you see here—a photographic tribute to Bob Marley.

Thanks belong to many of the folks who helped along the way:

Chris Murray of Govinda Gallery. The staff at Contact: Jeffrey Smith (thanks for spiriting this project), Robert Pledge, Audrey Jones, Samantha Box (thanks for fine digital care and handling), Dustin Ross, Ron Pledge, Bernice Koch, Dominique Deschavannes, Tim Mapp, Jacques Menashe, and Nancy Koch. Special thanks to Catherine Pledge, who has looked after my negatives for four decades, and to acclaimed producer Clive Chin for helping refresh my memory about all the talented musicians I met during my visit to Jamaica after many years. At *Time*: David DeVoss, then a *Time* correspondent, whose wisdom and wit helped me understand that journey; Arnold Drapkin, then *Time* picture editor who thought I was the right guy for that assignment.

And to my keenest critics, and best cheerleaders: Iris (Iree!) and Jordan Burnett, and Seth Jacobson, who regularly, and excitedly, lets me know when my pictures turn up at Nine Miles.

Chris Murray

To David Burnett, a brilliant photographer, a genuine gentleman, and a dear friend. Thank you, David, for your wonderful photos and stories of Jamaica and the reggae music scene. To Chris Salewicz, for his superb Foreword to this book. Jah Rastafari! To Barbara Genetin, for her sensitive and beautiful book design. To Jake Gerli, for keeping the ball rolling with this project. To Raoul Goff, may he be blessed with the love and wisdom of Jah. To David Murray at Govinda Gallery, for his expert research and organizational assistance with this book. Thank you to Meg Bowers, Julia Capalino, Sarah Leggin, and Molly Sciaretta at Govinda Gallery. To Jim Cassell, for his assistance editing the original transcripts. Jim, you are a gracious and long-time friend. To my queen Carlotta, for her positive vibrations. And most of all, to Bob Marley, for his everlasting spirit of love, freedom, and justice.

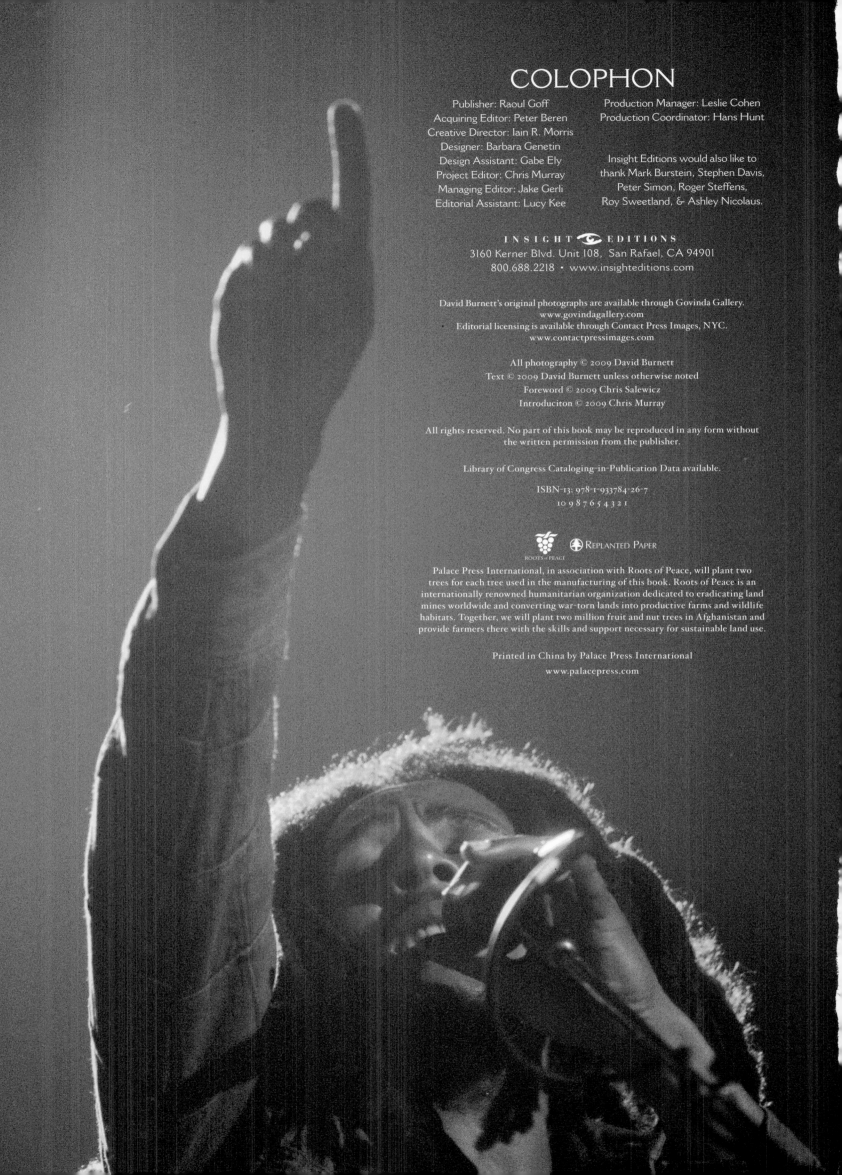

COLOPHON

Publisher: Raoul Goff
Acquiring Editor: Peter Beren
Creative Director: Iain R. Morris
Designer: Barbara Genetin
Design Assistant: Gabe Ely
Project Editor: Chris Murray
Managing Editor: Jake Gerli
Editorial Assistant: Lucy Kee

Production Manager: Leslie Cohen
Production Coordinator: Hans Hunt

Insight Editions would also like to
thank Mark Burstein, Stephen Davis,
Peter Simon, Roger Steffens,
Roy Sweetland, & Ashley Nicolaus.

INSIGHT EDITIONS
3160 Kerner Blvd. Unit 108, San Rafael, CA 94901
800.688.2218 • www.insighteditions.com

David Burnett's original photographs are available through Govinda Gallery.
www.govindagallery.com
Editorial licensing is available through Contact Press Images, NYC.
www.contactpressimages.com

Library of Congress Cataloging-in-Publication Data available.

ISBN-13: 978-1-933784-26-7
10 9 8 7 6 5 4 3 2 1

REPLANTED PAPER

ROOTS of PEACE

Palace Press International, in association with Roots of Peace, will plant two
trees for each tree used in the manufacturing of this book. Roots of Peace is an
internationally renowned humanitarian organization dedicated to eradicating land
mines worldwide and converting war-torn lands into productive farms and wildlife
habitats. Together, we will plant two million fruit and nut trees in Afghanistan and
provide farmers there with the skills and support necessary for sustainable land use.

Printed in China by Palace Press International
www.palacepress.com